KNOW YOUR GAME:

Basketball

MARC BLOOM

SCHOLASTIC INC.
New York Toronto London Auckland Sydney

Acknowledgment

Special thanks to Evan Pickman, PhD, associate professor of physical education at the College of Staten Island in New York. Pickman formerly coached basketball at CSI, is a past basketball director at Kutsher's Sports Academy in Monticello, New York, and currently serves as a scout for the Los Angeles Clippers of the NBA.

ISBN 0-590-43313-X

Design: Brian Collins
Illustrations: Joe Taylor

Designed and produced by Peter Elek Associates,
457 Broome Street, New York, NY 10013

12 11 10 9 8 7 6 5 4 3 2 1   0 1 2 3 4 5/9

Printed in the U.S.A.   23
First Scholastic printing, January 1991

Contents

Introduction

On almost every street in America, you can find a basketball hoop. It might be in someone's backyard, or attached to a pole, or in a playground. Just about everyone plays basketball while growing up.

Today, throughout the country, millions of people play basketball, attend games, and watch it on television. The sport has become almost as popular as baseball and football. It's also growing in popularity in other countries.

In the United States, college basketball, in particular, has drawn a lot of attention. The NCAA championship tournament, which concludes with The Final Four, is one of the year's biggest sports events.

Any young player can experience the excitement of basketball. The sport gives you a chance to learn new skills, exercise your body, play with friends, and perhaps be on a team as well.

This book will help you to enjoy basketball. It will explain how basketball is played and show you how to do your best at it.

You probably know a little about basketball from playing with friends. Maybe you're even a member of a school or recreation team. Or perhaps you've attended high school games or watched basketball on television.

No matter what you may already know about basketball, there is much more to learn. The more you know about the game, the more you'll develop as a player, and the better you'll like it.

In this book, you'll read about basketball skills, rules, gear, and teamwork. Most of what you read will be about team play on a full court. You'll also find out how to get in shape for basketball, how to set goals for yourself, and how to build up your confidence.

As you'll see, you don't have to be tall to play basketball and enjoy it. For young players, height is not important. Good players come in all sizes. What is important is to try your best and learn all you can about the game.

Chapter 1

Having Fun

If you follow basketball, you've probably seen interviews on television with professional star Magic Johnson of the Los Angeles Lakers. He's always got a big smile on his face. Whether his team wins or loses, Magic has a great time. He loves the game, and it shows.

Anyone who plays basketball can have as much fun at it as Magic does. Having fun means feeling good about how you play the game. It means knowing you tried your best, and enjoying yourself with your friends.

At the end of every game, you should be able to smile, too. You should be able to tell everyone, "I did my best. It was a good game. I look forward to the next one."

One of the nice things about basketball is that every player on the court gets the chance to handle the ball on almost every play. Teamwork is stressed. With only five people playing at once, the ball must be moved around by a team to be successful.

Every player is allowed to shoot, too, to score points. Shooting with accuracy adds to the fun of a game.

In basketball, people think that if you're tall, you're automatically a great player. After all, almost all of the college and pro players are well over 6 feet; some top 7 feet!

However, there are many tall athletes who don't make very good basketball players. That is because they don't use their size well.

Using your size means knowing how to position your body on the court to gain an advantage over the other team. There's an expression coaches use about players. "He plays taller than he is," they'll say, as a compliment. That means a player who's 5'6" might position himself so well it seems he or she is 6 feet tall.

Basketball can be fun for many different reasons. These reasons include: being a member of a team, learning sportsmanship, developing skills, getting healthful exercise, and playing with rules. Also, it's fun having a coach, increasing your self-confidence, and feeling proud to wear an athletic uniform.

Being a Member of a Team

Basketball gyms are small compared with baseball, football, and soccer fields. When you play on a basketball team, the spectators are seated very close to the court. Every player is in the spotlight.

On a team, you'll learn to play together with kids your own age. You'll learn how to handle the ball with team success in mind. And you'll realize a team that relies on one star player usually does not do well.

Don't feel you must join a team right away. When you play on your own with friends, you have more freedom on the court than in a team game with extra rules.

7

Decide which you like better. If you do join a team, you must attend practice sessions, listen to the coach, and try to learn as much about the game as possible.

Learning Sportsmanship

Professional athletes do not always show good sportsmanship. In basketball, however, there are excellent examples. You've probably seen games in which one player pats an opposing player on the back after they've collided on a rough play.

It's important for players to show respect for one another. That's part of what sportsmanship is about. Isiah Thomas is certainly one player who shows this respect. When his team, the Detroit Pistons, played the 1989 NBA championship against the Los Angeles Lakers, Thomas congratulated Lakers' star Magic Johnson after each game.

Above all else, sportsmanship means playing with fairness. It means doing what the coach asks of you, and not being a "sore loser" if things don't turn out the way you'd like.

Sportsmanship also involves thinking of the feelings of other players. During the 1989-90 season, a dispute arose over a record-breaking high school performance that some people say was inconsiderate of the losing team.

Lisa Leslie of Morningside High in Inglewood, California, broke the state record by scoring 101 points in a game against South Torrence High. Toward the end of the game, with Morningside ahead, the South Torrence coach took his team and left the court. He felt

Morningside had unfairly "run up the score" just to break a record and had taken advantage of his weaker team.

Developing Skills

In a way, basketball appears to be a very simple game. The object is clear: Get the ball in the basket. But there is much to learn about skills like dribbling and passing, and also about each situation that can develop in a game.

All players, no matter what position they may specialize in, need to learn the basics of the game. Coaches call these the game's fundamentals.

Try to become a complete player. You'll need to learn all aspects of basketball in order to play the game well. Even guards need to learn rebounding; centers must learn to dribble. As you grow and your body changes, you may be assigned a different position. A coach may feel your size and skills are better suited to another position on the court.

Getting Healthful Exercise

There is no sport that will get you as physically fit as basketball. You move constantly and utilize all the parts of your body during the game. At times, you'll feel your heart beating like a drum. That shows you're really getting a terrific workout.

Coaches use practices both to teach skills and to instill good habits about being in shape. There's no way to play an "easy" game of basketball.

All this movement is good for you, too. It builds

strength and stamina. When you're in good shape and in good health, you feel you're at your best in sports. If you feel sluggish on the court, it could be that you have not done enough to get physically fit.

Playing With Rules

Without rules, basketball would be disorganized and dangerous. Rules are necessary for your protection and for your enjoyment of the game. They are enforced by referees.

Just as you learn how to dribble and pass, you must learn the rules of basketball and follow them. Even during pickup games with friends, it makes sense to pay attention to certain key rules. Some rules involve body contact. Others concern the use of the court and the way the game is set up.

Having a Coach

Ever notice how different coaches behave during a game? Some sit on the bench and barely say a word. Others get very excited, giving players instructions and pacing up and down the sideline. Just as players have different personalities, so do coaches. Some yell and scream; others speak quietly. Some go over their pointers again and again . . . and again. Others say something once, and that's it. But as long as a coach treats you fairly, you should feel satisfied.

A coach is a teacher of basketball. He or she should help you learn the game and enjoy it. If, for any reason, you feel a coach is not being fair with you, tell your parents. Parents are supposed to be involved with their childrens' teams; they should be able to speak with your coach about how you're doing.

Increasing Self-confidence

Michael Jordan of the Chicago Bulls, probably the greatest basketball player in the game today, did not always have the confidence he now shows on the court. Michael's main sports were baseball and football, but he was determined to excel in basketball, too. All he needed was a little more confidence.

Michael practiced hard and improved his skills. He became a better player and a more confident one, too. With skills and confidence, he was on his way.

Most athletes lack confidence when they begin a sport or test themselves against highly skilled players.

Succeeding in one aspect of basketball will give you confidence in other parts of the game. You may even find yourself becoming a more confident person in general. Through sports, you learn how much you can achieve when you put your mind to something.

Pride in the Uniform

Your reward for working hard in practice is a sharp-looking uniform with a number on it. With your fellow players suited up, everyone will have a lot of team spirit.

For each game, remember to be alert and follow the coach's instructions. Try your best and, win or lose, take pride in earning the privilege to play on a basketball team.

11

Chapter 2
Basketball Rules

When basketball is played in a backyard or playground, it may seem as though there are no rules at all. Everyone scrambles for the ball. The court is small. The hoop may not even have a net or much of a backboard. When the players get tired, they call it quits.

But even in those informal games there are plenty of rules. How many players on each side? How many points for each basket? How many baskets win the game? You cannot play a basketball game without some rules.

Rules prevent any player or team from having an unfair advantage. Rules also keep the activity safe and make sure the game is played with discipline. In basketball, discipline means playing with control instead of being wild on the court.

In organized team play, referees enforce the rules. They wear striped shirts and stand out on the court. They are called "refs" for short. When a foul is committed, the ref blows a whistle and uses hand signals to describe the foul and the penalty given.

Once a ref has made a decision, it stands. You can be further penalized if you argue with the ref.

In basketball, many rules are the same whether you play in a youth league or on a professional team. The more you know about the rules, the better a player you can become. Here are some of basketball's most important rules:

1. *The court:* An NBA court measures 94 feet long and 50 feet wide. College courts usually are the same size. High school courts are slightly smaller—no bigger than 84 feet by 50 feet. Youth games may be played on courts roughly 60 feet long and 40 feet wide.

2. *The basket:* An official basket is made of metal and measures 18 inches around the rim (this is called the circumference). It is 10 feet high and has an open net attached to it.

3. *The basketball:* A standard basketball measures roughly 30 inches around. All girls' leagues and youth teams use a slightly smaller ball.

4. *Scoring:* A basket can be scored whether the ball hits the backboard first (called a banked shot), bounces on the rim, or goes right through the net without touching the rim (known as a "swish").

5. *Teams:* Five players on each side start a game. Most teams have between twelve and fifteen players altogether.

6. *Substitutes:* When a player enters the game as a substitute (or "sub"), it is known as "coming off the bench." In youth play, every team member has to play at least a part of the game.

7. *Referee:* Every game has at least one referee. College and pro games have two or three refs. Referees are also called umpires.

8. *Start of play:* A game is started by a jump ball. Each team's tallest player (or best jumper) stands at the middle of the court. The other players are posi-

tioned around them a few steps away. The ref tosses the ball in the air between the two jumpers. They leap to tap the ball in the direction of a teammate.

9. *Offense:* The team that has the ball and tries to score a basket.

10. *Defense:* The team without the ball that tries to prevent the other team from scoring and attempts to regain possession of the ball.

11. *Field goal:* Other than a free throw, when a basket is made, it is called a field goal or a shot "from the floor." It scores two points, unless it was made from beyond the three-point line.

12. *Three-pointer:* A shot that is made from the basket that earns three points. There is a curved line marking three-point territory. In the pros, it is 23 feet 9 inches from the basket. In high school and college, it's 19 feet 9 inches away. Youth leagues may have a shorter three-point line.

13. *Foul line:* The foul line is 15 feet from the basket. A player shooting a foul shot must stay behind the foul line.

14. *Free throw:* If a foul is committed, a team may be awarded one or two free shots from the foul line.

15. *Fouls:* Most of the time, fouls are called when a player charges into another player (also called charging), or pushes a player, or hits his or her arm while the player is shooting the ball (sometimes called hacking).

16. *Technical foul:* When a player or coach has shown unsportsmanlike conduct, the ref can call a technical foul, giving the other team two free throws.

14

17. *Dribbling:* Dribbling must be done one hand at a time, with either hand. You cannot dribble with both hands at the same time. Once you stop dribbling, you must shoot or pass.

18. *Traveling:* While holding the ball, generally you are allowed to take one step with it. If you take an extra step, it is considered traveling, and the ball is turned over to the other team. This is also known as "walking" or taking "steps."

19. *Goaltending:* If there's a shot moving downward that looks like it is going in the basket and a defensive player reaches up and hits it away, it is goaltending. If this happens, the shot counts as a score.

20. *Screens:* A player may "screen" for a teammate by standing between the teammate and a defensive player, serving as a blocker. The player screening cannot hit or bump the defensive player while moving around.

21. *Game time:* The NBA plays four 12-minute quarters (or periods) for a total of 48 minutes per game. Colleges play two 20-minute halves, a total of 40 minutes a game. High school teams usually play four 8-minute quarters.

22. *Shot clock:* In the NBA, a team has 24 seconds to take a first shot. In most college conferences, a team has 45 seconds to get a shot off. Some high school leagues and youth teams also use a shot clock. High school girls' teams use a 30-second shot clock.

23. *Overtime:* Ties are broken by overtime periods. These periods are 5 minutes in college and the pros

15

but only 3 minutes in high school.

24. *Fouling out:* If one player commits a given number of fouls, he or she "fouls out" and is forced to leave the game. In college, a player fouls out after committing five fouls; in the NBA, it's six.

25. *Clothing:* Regulation uniforms must be worn in team games. For safety reasons, jewelry of any kind is not allowed. (For more on gear, see chapter 5.)

Chapter 3
Basketball Skills

Basketball stars are big celebrities, and young players like to try to imitate their fancy moves on the court. What kids don't realize is that the champions are great players because they can perform the basic skills, not only the flashy ones, with perfection.

Don't think you're going to be another Michael Jordan. At least, not yet. Don't be concerned with behind-the-back passes, slam dunks, or sky hooks. Young players must learn the fundamentals first.

Good players at any level do their jobs on the court, make few mistakes, and are excellent team players. They develop their own style of play and don't try to copy others.

In basketball, there are seven basic skills to concentrate on. They are: (1) basic body position, (2) dribbling,(3) passing, (4) catching, (5) shooting, (6) rebounding, and (7) defense.

Basic Body Position

Most movement in basketball is best done from the same low body position. This position gives you balance and power. It helps you to move in every direction and get the jump on your opponent.

Spread your feet apart, slightly more than shoulder width. Crouch down a little by bending your

knees. Keep your back straight. Don't bend at the hips. Put your weight on the balls of your feet, and don't lean on one foot. Make sure your weight is even so your right and left sides feel "equal."

In this position, you'll be able to become what coaches call a "triple threat." Whenever you get the ball, you'll be ready to dribble, pass, or shoot. The defense won't know what to expect.

Dribbling

Another quality of an effective player is the ability to dribble equally well with either hand. This skill will improve your game enormously. You'll be able to cut toward the basket on both the right and left sides of the court. This is known as "going both ways."

Most coaches feel that players of any age can

18

begin to practice dribbling with both hands. Make sure you practice with your weaker hand. Be patient; it can take years to become equally good with either hand.

When dribbling, don't let your palm touch the ball. Spread your hand, keep it cupped, and touch the ball with your fingers. There should be some space between your palm and the ball. Your hand should be relaxed.

When you bounce the ball, push it firmly by snapping your wrist. Don't slap at the ball. Keep your hand over the ball and don't let it bounce higher than your waist.

As you're dribbling, remember to keep your knees bent, back straight, and feet spread apart. Lean forward a bit, keeping your chin up. And don't look at the

19

ball—look up to see to whom you should pass. Try to get the feel of the ball.

When guarded closely by the defense, you'll have to dribble a little lower and to the side to keep control of the ball. Use your free arm to keep the defender away. In the open court, by yourself, you can dribble the ball higher and in front of you.

According to NBA All-Star guard John Stockton of the Utah Jazz, you should first practice dribbling in place. Then, dribble as you walk. After that, try dribbling as you run. Push the ball a stride ahead of you, letting it bounce high but no higher than your waist.

When Stockton was a young player, he would practice dribbling in his basement with the lights turned off. He was forced to get the feel of the ball because he could not see it.

Passing

Passing is the key to basketball. You may have heard the expression, "Hit the open man." The easy

pass to an open player is best—and it usually works. Don't get fancy.

A pass can be done with one or both hands. It can be made on a bounce or a fly. The ball can be pushed, tossed, lobbed, or thrown like a baseball. As with dribbling, use your fingers, not your palm, to control the ball and make your passes crisp.

The chest pass is the one you'll use most of the time. It's the most reliable. Hold the ball at your chest with your thumbs behind the ball. Step toward the player you're throwing to and push the ball from your chest. As you release the ball, snap your wrists to give it good speed.

Catching

A pass works only if the ball is caught. It's easy to miss catching a pass if you're not alert or moving in the wrong direction. The first rule of catching a pass is: Be ready for it.

Keep your hands open and your fingers spread apart. Use both hands, unless the ball is thrown off to one side. Have your palms facing the ball. When you catch the ball, tighten your grip on it and move the ball to the side so it can't be smacked out of your hands.

Try to guess what your teammates will do with the ball. And even though you should stay in a crouched position so you can step to the ball with quickness and balance, make yourself as large a target as possible by raising your arms.

Shooting

Just because there's a three-point shot, don't think you have to learn to shoot the long bombs. "Learn to hit from 5 to 8 feet, then move out," advises Ed Badger, former head coach of the Chicago Bulls of the NBA.

Again, use your fingers on the ball. Keep your elbows in to give your shot direction. Hold the ball in your shooting hand but keep it secure with your other hand until you're about to shoot.

Don't throw the ball at the basket. Push the ball up with the snap of your wrist so it rolls off your fingers. And reach up to give the shot good height. If a shot has a curve, or arc, to it, it has a better chance of going in.

Shoot the ball softly so it floats to the basket. That way, even if it hits the rim it might bounce in. This is known as having a soft touch.

22

Also, look at the rim as you shoot. A good shooter does not see the ball until it's in the air on the way down.

In shooting, your hands do not do all the work. Your feet and legs help out. Keep your feet spread apart and facing the basket so you'll be "square" with it. And bend your knees. The strength in your legs helps you reach the basket with your shot.

If you're close to the basket, you have the choice of "banking" your shot off the backboard. Use the lower part of the backboard—the box on the "glass"—and aim carefully at it without looking at the basket. Tap the ball lightly off the backboard so it falls in. A forceful shot could bounce away.

You should rely on the backboard for most layups. Layups are shots taken as you dribble up to the basket. You must control the ball as you stop dribbling and lay the ball up toward the backboard with one foot off the ground. The ball should roll gently off your fingers.

Players of high-school age and up do much of their shooting with jump shots. At age eleven or twelve, you can begin to work on your jumper.

Many players tend to jump in the air first, then shoot, in two separate movements. It's better to shoot in one continuous move by releasing the ball as your feet leave the ground. You'll get your shot off more quickly and have greater power.

One shot that some players take for granted is a free throw. They think it's a breeze because it's "free"— no one guards you and there's time to set it up. However, the free throw line is 15 feet from the basket. That's a long shot for a young player.

Shoot it like a standard shot. First, however, take a deep breath to relax. Don't rush the shot. When you're ready, bend your knees, make sure your toes are behind the line, and concentrate.

As you shoot, lift your heels off the floor so your whole body drives the shot toward the basket. Follow through with your shooting arm so your palm faces the ground after the ball is released and your index finger points straight down.

There's no shortcut to good foul shooting. You simply have to practice it over and over again, just like you must practice all your shots.

A shooting drill recommended by former college basketball coach Evan Pickman is to lie on your back and "shoot" the ball up in the air a few feet high. If the ball continues to come down right to you, you know you've been accurate with your shots.

Rebounding

The best jumpers are not always the strongest rebounders. In regaining the ball after a shot that's been missed, it's important to get good position under the basket and to be aggressive.

Getting good position involves "boxing out" your opponent by trying to position yourself between the basket and the opposing player. You must use your

body to maneuver in front of the player.

When your team has the ball, you'll try to rebound a missed shot so that you can take a shot yourself. When the other team has the ball, a rebound will give your team the ball to move offensively toward the other basket.

Basic body position for rebounding is crucial. By crouching with knees bent and with your weight on the front of the feet, you'll be able to explode toward the ball. Also, by keeping your elbows out, you'll make it harder for your opponent to get around you. The "bigger" you stand, the harder it is to be outmaneuvered. The idea is to take up as much space as possible.

Defense

When guarding a player with the ball, you'll do a lot of side-to-side movement. You must stick to the

offensive player like glue. As you move sideways (called lateral movement), keep your feet wide apart for balance and quickness.

The player with the ball may try to change directions quickly. With a wide stance, you'll be able to follow those moves. Don't slouch or let your legs cross.

Try to prevent the offense from making good passes. At times, you may have a chance to steal the ball or block a shot. You must do everything you can to prevent a score.

Show a coach you like to play defense, and you'll earn his or her respect as a team player. As a high school freshman, Kareem Abdul-Jabbar knew that. "He always wanted to guard the opposing team's best player. He was not afraid of a challenge," says Dick Percudani, a pro scout who coached Jabbar as a high school freshman in New York City.

Together with quick feet, you need quick hands. To steal the ball, instead of lunging with your body, slash out with your hands. "Like a snake's tongue," is how one coach describes it.

On defense, there are two main types of team formation: one-to-one play, and zone defense. You'll find out more about both formations in the next chapter.

Chapter 4
Basketball Teamwork

In basketball, teamwork is so important that there are players with reputations for their great passing. One is Larry Bird of the Boston Celtics. He can thread the needle with his passes. And when he does, the Celtics usually win.

"Even if you're a good shooter, don't become selfish with the ball," says former Chicago Bulls coach Ed Badger, who at one time worked with the Celtics. "Larry Bird never takes a shot if someone else has a better one."

If you "hog" the ball by dribbling or shooting too much, you won't be helping your team. You won't be improving your own play, either. Players get better by working the ball around the court to their teammates. The object of your offense is to score. It does not matter which player makes the shot.

Usually, if a team plays a good game, each player will get a chance to do a little of everything: dribble, pass, grab a few rebounds, score some points. However, only five players from a team take the court at once. That's not many compared to nine in baseball, eleven in football, and eleven in soccer.

That means most of a team's players sit on the bench for portions of the game. They are brought in as substitutes, but a few may not play very much. If a

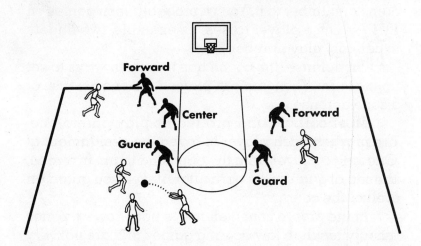

player is new to the game, he or she can learn a lot just by sitting on the bench and watching the action.

Benchwarmers help the team, too. They provide team spirit by encouraging other players. And when they do come into the game, even for a few minutes, they are just as important as the starting players. The coach puts them at certain positions and asks them to perform specific jobs, or roles, based on their size, skills, and experience.

These roles are what basketball is all about. A team relies on each player doing his or her job. When players work together in basketball, it's an amazing thing to watch.

The offensive team can call a "set" play or just move the ball around until one player is clear for a good shot. A set play is one that you practice before-hand and try to execute in a game. It might have a name or number to it. You've probably seen games on TV in which a player raises, for example, two fingers to call for "play number 2."

On defense, the coach has two main ways to set up the team. The team can play one-to-one defense or a zone defense.

Most college and pro teams play one-to-one. That's when each player is given the assignment of guarding a player from the opposing team. In a zone, instead of guarding a particular player, you guard an area of the court.

In the pros, a zone defense is not allowed. Zones usually result in low-scoring games that are not very exciting. The pros like action-packed, high-scoring games because they draw larger crowds, and more people will watch them on TV.

Another defensive tactic is a full-court press. Instead of waiting for the offensive team to bring the ball past mid-court, the defense "attacks" as soon as the ball is put into play. Defenders try to upset the offense and steal the ball.

No matter what your favorite position happens to be, you should know the role of each player and how they work together as a unit on both offense and defense. Basically there are only three different positions in basketball: guard, forward, and center.

Guard

Guards usually are smaller players who can move quickly. They receive the ball first and bring it up the court to the other players. Guards handle the ball a lot and must be excellent dribblers.

There are two guard positions. Sometimes, guards share the duties of bringing the ball up. Other times, one guard takes charge and might be called a point guard.

A point guard is like a quarterback. He or she sets up players and serves as a leader. The guard keeps a team's movement flowing toward the basket. At times, guards talk to their teammates during play, directing them to move in a certain way.

Guards must be able to think fast once they get possession of the ball. Should you dribble, pass to a nearby teammate, or make a long pass up the court?

Guards also determine the pace of play. They decide whether to move the ball slowly or quickly; at times, they'll try to start a "fast break."

In a successful fast break, the offense catches the defense out of position. While bringing the ball up the court, the offense is ready to work a play before the defense has a chance to set up. Perhaps a defensive player is tired and lagging down court. When this happens, the offense sees an advantage and races with the ball. By moving the ball quickly, the offense should have a player in the open for an easy shot.

For a fast break to succeed, the offense must be able to dribble, pass, and shoot on the run. Coaches have teams practice this. Guards learn to sense how their teammates will move on a fast break.

As you can see, guards must do a lot on the court. They must be versatile. They should be triple threats—able to dribble, pass, and shoot. They should

31

also learn to "screen" by blocking a defender from reaching a player with the ball. This is also known as "setting a pick."

By moving around, guards force other players to move, too. Continuous movement is the way to get a player open and away from the defense. Then you have an easier shot.

When dribbling, guards should face the basket as much as possible. If you're pressured by the defense, it's natural to turn around with your back to the basket in order to protect the ball. Learn to face forward, or sideways, using your free arm to keep the defender away. This way you'll be able to see your teammates and know to whom to pass. The ability to dribble well with either hand is a tremendous advantage.

Guards have to make sure their teammates are spread out properly. Two players should never stand next to one another waiting for something to happen. That makes it easier for the defense to guard them.

A guard who really knows the game is a player who makes his teammates look good. By passing effectively, guards enable forwards and centers to have easier shots and a chance to score.

On defense, guards work in the reverse. They try to block passes, steal the ball, and force the offense to lose the ball on turnovers. They must always be ready to get the ball back and make the "transition" to offensive play.

Forward

Forwards play in the corners but move around a

lot. They should be able to hit baskets from the 10–12 foot range. Most of the top NBA scorers are forwards, including Larry Bird of the Celtics.

To be an effective shooter, you have to learn many different moves. If you shoot the same way every time, the defense will have an easy time guarding you.

From the corners, you have to move with the ball and without it. Moving without the ball involves cutting in different directions to get open and receive a pass. Sometimes you have to fake one way, then dart another to get free.

Forwards don't dribble that much, but they pass a lot. They trade passes with the guards, or dish the ball off to the center. If the center is not clear, don't force a pass into the middle or it'll probably get stolen.

At times, forwards need to penetrate the middle of the court. Forwards who can muscle their way to the basket are called power forwards. Some, like Charles Barkley of the Philadelphia 76ers, seem almost unstoppable. Other forwards rely more on their outside shot to score.

In order to provide the guards with a target for passes, forwards sometimes play with their backs to the basket. This is called "playing the post." Using the basic squat, you try to get in front of the defensive player, stand your ground, and extend your arms to grab a pass. Then, you can try to curl around the player guarding you with a move to the basket.

Or, you can try for a quick turnaround jumpshot. First, fake a move to the basket, drawing the defender off balance, then shoot. After shooting, in case you miss, follow up your shot by rushing in for the rebound.

On defense, forwards try to avoid getting stuck behind a post, or screen, or getting beat to a rebound. You must let the offense know you mean business, and you will not allow yourself to be pushed around. You have to make them work hard. You have to play good defense.

Center

On many teams, the tallest player is put at center, but only if the player can be aggressive. If you're not able to use your strength against defenders, you'll be outplayed again and again.

Centers put a lot of energy into getting into proper position. They play in the middle, up near the basket. However, because of the three-second rule, offensive players are not allowed to just station themselves in the middle.

That means centers must move around to get open for a pass. It also means that when a center plays a post and does stand in one place for a few seconds, he or she must be positioned outside the three-second zone.

Centers can play a low post or high post. When they play in low, they're closer to the basket. On a high post, the center can be way up near the foul line.

Playing high, centers can feed guards cutting to the basket. On the low post, they can try for short, "high-percentage" shots, tip-ins, layups—anything that works.

34

As a center, you need good footwork. Because they're tall and strong, centers draw extra defensive coverage from players who double-team them. Centers must be agile enough to get off shots in heavy traffic.

Also, as the team's key rebounder, the center must be an expert in boxing out and fight hard for rebounds. When they get a defensive rebound, centers should make sure they have control of the ball. Then, they should make a quick "outlet" pass to a guard who will set up the next play.

On transition to offense, centers should not lag downcourt. After grabbing a rebound and pass, they should hustle up to their position and be ready.

Chapter 5
Basketball Gear

One of the best things about basketball is that you hardly need any equipment at all. A ball, a basket, and a pair of sneakers should do it. You don't even need a friend. You can play by yourself and have plenty of fun.

Most of the top college and professional players began shooting hoops on neighborhood courts. The baskets probably didn't have nets or much of a backboard. Most likely, players suited up in any old sweatshirt they had around.

As stars, they now dress up for every game. If you've watched basketball on TV, you may have noticed the many types of clothing teams use.

If you join a team, you'll probably get a uniform to wear. You may even receive a warm-up sweatshirt. It won't be as fancy as what the stars have, but you'll be awfully proud to show it off.

You may have to return it at the end of the season, or you may have a chance to buy it. Any gear that you do need for basketball can be purchased at most sporting goods stores. Here's a look at some basketball gear:

Basketball: Balls differ slightly in size, color, and in the materials from which they're made. A standard ball measures 29-1/2 to 30 inches around, and weighs twenty to twenty-two ounces (a little less than one and a half pounds). College and high-school-aged girls use a ball that measures 28-1/2 to 29 inches around, and weighs eighteen to twenty ounces.

Some balls are considered indoor balls, while others are better for outdoor use. It depends on what the outer part of the ball is made of. Leather balls are better for gym floors. But leather will scrape on an outdoor, concrete surface. Outdoor balls have a more durable plastic coating that won't get cut up. Certain types of balls may be fine for either indoor or outdoor play.

There are also small-sized balls for young players. They are easier to handle and are good for practice if you're just learning the game.

Basketball pump: With use, a basketball loses air. It's like a tire: Every so often, you have to pump it up. Balls have tiny holes in them for this purpose. You pump air into the ball through this hole.

Baskets: A portable hoop, net, and backboard will give you a convenient way to practice at home. They are easily assembled and can be installed in a backyard or driveway. There are two types: those that are attached to a wall, such as outside a garage, and those that come with a pole.

The baskets can be set at regulation 10-foot height or at lower heights for beginning players.

Sneakers: There are many types of basketball sneakers to choose from. Many are fancy and expensive. They have become popular because of TV commercials in which star players are shown wearing them. While they may be "cool," they won't make you a better player.

Sneakers should have thick soles and feel sturdy and comfortable. Sneakers should give you support. They should cushion your feet when you run and jump on hard, wooden courts. If your sneakers don't provide enough support, you could injure your feet or legs.

Sneakers fall into two main categories: half-sneakers and high-tops. Most players wear high-tops because they come up over the ankles and may prevent your ankles from twisting and getting hurt. Some players who prefer half-sneakers feel they're lighter and easier to run in. Every player has to decide which kind feels better.

Clothing: Team uniforms have a matching shirt and shorts. The shirt is usually sleeveless, also called a tank top. It will have the team name or nickname on it, a number, and maybe your own name, too. Some players feel comfortable wearing a regular T-shirt under their uniform shirt.

Wear thick athletic socks that come up above the ankle. For added support, you can wear an extra pair of socks. There are high socks that come up close to the knee.

Knee pads: Many players wear knee pads for added protection in case they fall. Some types of padding are not allowed in certain leagues because they're made of hard material and could hurt someone.

Water bottle: Try to have a plastic water bottle with you if you'll be playing for a long while. Fill it with cold water and ice or a sports drink. This is important in warm weather, but a good idea even when it's cool. Running around builds up a strong thirst. If you don't drink water after sweating, you can get sick.

Safety rules: Jewelry, such as watches, rings, necklaces, and earrings, must be removed before a game. Playing with any sharp object on your body can hurt others or cause harm to yourself.

Eyeglasses: In most youth leagues, you are allowed to play in eyeglasses. You can also wear contact lenses. To be safer, buy protective goggles that fit over your glasses. Kareem Abdul-Jabbar wore them for many years in the NBA. There are now prescription goggles being made. If you wear glasses, you might want to try them out.

Chapter 6
Basketball Conditioning

The next time you play basketball on your own, try the following test to see what kind of shape you're in. Take a few shots from the outside. Run up and down the court several times. Then shoot again.

How do you feel on the second bunch of shots? Are you alert and relaxed, or weak and out of breath? If the second set of shots feel more difficult than the first, don't be too upset. You're like a lot of young players—you don't get enough exercise and lack physical conditioning.

Playing basketball is one of the best sports for getting in shape. But it won't get you in shape unless you play with energy. Just shooting around is not enough. Coaches believe you should use your everyday playing to help get yourself in condition for team games. "You should practice sometimes against players who are better than you. It forces you to work harder," suggests Dick McGuire, a scout for the New York Knicks.

Your greatest obstacle on the court is not the player guarding you. It's fatigue. Once you get tired, you won't play as hard. A player who's tired cannot concentrate. You lose your balance, use incorrect form, and trip more often. You increase risk of injury, and you'll be too exhausted to use the skills you practiced and learned.

Even top players need to work at being in shape. That's why the pros have training camps. Basketball players need to limber up, work their muscles, perhaps even lose some weight, in order to run, shoot, rebound, dribble—do everything necessary to succeed on the court.

If you have not played much basketball, physical fitness can help you make up for lack of skills. By hustling, you'll outplay your slower opponents. You won't cave in toward the end of a game. Coaches like to see players able to zip around the court late in a game.

Coaches use many types of drills on the court to get players in shape. You can do some of them on your own or with friends. Sometimes you use the ball; other times you don't.

Here's one without the ball. On a full-court, stand at the baseline under a basket. Run to the foul line, then back to the baseline. Then, run to the mid-court line and back to the baseline. Then, run to the foul line on the other side and back to the baseline. Finally, run clear across court to the other baseline and back to where you started from.

Don't pause to rest between runs. Keep going until you've completed the course.

This drill not only develops speed and stamina but also your ability to quickly change directions. There's a trick to doing it correctly so that you'll also make sharper moves in a game.

Don't go all-out on each run. If you do, you'll be off balance every time you have to stop and reverse direction. Run fast, but hold back a little. As you approach each turning line, slow down, shorten your steps, touch the line quickly, then dash the other way.

You have to move like that all the time in games. How you time your footwork is as important as how much speed you have.

Try the same type of drill with a ball. Dribble as you run. Keep the ball under control. When you're near a basket, take a shot. Remember to use correct body position and look up at all times.

For another drill that involves dribbling and shooting, stand at the foul line on a full court. Take a foul shot. Then, retrieve the ball and dribble to the foul line on the other side. Take another shot. Get the ball again, and continue using both sides of the court for a total of ten shots or more.

That will give you the feel of game conditions. You can do this with a buddy by starting on opposite ends of the court. Have fun by trying to keep pace with one another and sink baskets. Don't forget to do some dribbling with your weaker hand.

Experienced athletes know that each part of the body affects another part. Sit-ups will strengthen your stomach muscles. Try to do 25 to 50 sit-ups every day. Do them slowly, keeping your knees bent. Also try to do some stretching exercises on a regular basis. Most coaches and sports doctors agree that young players should not use weights until they're at least sixteen. Instead, for strength, do push-ups and chin-ups.

When you feel yourself getting in shape, try that simple shooting test again. Take a few shots, run the court several times, then shoot again. This time, the shots probably will feel a lot easier.

Chapter 7

Basketball Organization and Stars

In the winter of 1891, a physical education teacher named James Naismith of Springfield, Massachusetts, decided to try a new activity with his students. One day he walked into the school gymnasium and attached a basket used to collect peaches to a balcony about 10 feet high. He handed a soccer ball to the boys in his class, and they began to toss it around and throw it into the basket.

And so the game of basketball was born, roughly one hundred years ago. Naismith is considered the "father" of basketball. Today, the Basketball Hall of Fame is named after Naismith and located in Springfield.

The first organized games were not actually played until 1892. Teams were formed at YMCAs, and colleges began to take up the sport. A few years later, as the game became popular, the Amateur Athletic Union (AAU) helped the sport to grow across the country.

Soon there were also professional teams, teams sponsored by businesses for their workers, women's teams, and high school teams. An exhibition basketball tournament was held at the 1904 Olympic Games in St. Louis, Missouri.

Naismith's peach baskets did not last very long. Wire mesh baskets replaced them, but they had no hole at the bottom. The open net did not come into use until 1906.

In 1939, the National College Athletic Association (NCAA) held its first championship. Pro basketball struggled until three leagues joined in 1949 to form the National Basketball Association (NBA). The league had seventeen teams then. Under coach Red Auerbach, the Boston Celtics won nine NBA titles in ten years. The Celtics' star center was Bill Russell, a great defensive player. In the 1960s, a fierce rivalry developed between the league's two best big men—the 6'10" Russell, and 7'1" Wilt "the Stilt" Chamberlain of Philadelphia.

Chamberlain became the game's greatest scorer. He is the only player ever to score 100 points in an NBA game. In the college ranks, the University of California at Los Angeles (UCLA) was almost unbeatable. Coached by John Wooden, the Bruins won the NCAA title ten straight years, from 1964 through 1973. Since then, no team has even won it twice in a row.

For four years during that period, the Bruins were led by a 7'2" center, Kareem Abdul-Jabbar. Jabbar first became known to basketball fans as an outstanding teenage player in New York City. His name was not Jabbar then. It was Lewis Alcindor. Because of his belief in the Muslim faith, Alcindor changed his name.

After college, Jabbar went on to star in the NBA. He played a record 20 seasons, retiring in 1989 at the age of forty-two. He is the NBA's all-time scoring leader.

The NBA has gradually expanded. Now it has 27 teams. An important milestone occurred in 1977, when the American Basketball Association (ABA) folded, and a number of its teams were taken into the NBA.

The ABA existed from 1968 to 1976. Its top player, Julius Irving, known as "Dr. J", also starred in the NBA. He thrilled fans with his spectacular high-flying leaps to the basket. It seemed as though he could float in the air, defying gravity. In basketball, this action is called "hang time."

Today, the king of hang time is Michael Jordan of the Chicago Bulls. Along with Larry Bird of the Celtics and Magic Johnson of the Lakers, Jordan is one of the NBA's three best players. He's certainly the most exciting. No one can fly around the court like Jordan.

Though women have been playing basketball almost as long as men have, basketball did not become an official college championship sport for women until 1975. Women's games are on television, and they have a Final Four, too. The top female player in the history of the game, Cheryl Miller, led the University of Southern California (USC) to back-to-back NCAA titles in 1983–1984.

However, there has not been a successful pro league for women in the U.S. A few leagues sprung up but eventually folded. Today none exist. Some women have continued their careers by going to other countries, like Italy, where there is professional basketball for women.

Here are the different branches of the sport:

Youth Leagues

Most community recreation programs feature basketball. There are also YMCA programs, as well as basketball opportunities through such groups as the Catholic Youth Organization (CYO) and Jewish Community Center (JCC).

Other programs include Biddy Basketball for youngsters twelve and under. This is a program involving more than 17,000 boys and girls nationwide. The basket stands 8½ feet high, instead of 10 feet, and the ball is smaller—27 or 28 inches. Teams play six-minute quarters.

Amateur Athletic Union (AAU)

The AAU conducts many sports programs for young athletes. It includes basketball for boys (nineteen and under) and girls (eighteen and under). There are AAU associations all over the country. To play, you must join the AAU. Teams play a regular season, then try to qualify for the annual national championship tournament.

High School

Virtually every high school has basketball teams for boys and girls. Along with football, basketball is considered the major high school sport. Games are written up in newspapers, and top players become

47

known as possible pros of the future. These young stars play in all-star games and may receive athletic scholarships to college.

Amateur Basketball Association of the USA

The ABAUSA, as it is called, selects the national teams that will compete in various international tournaments, such as those at the Olympic Games and Pan American Games. In the past, U.S. teams were made up primarily of college players. But a new rule now allows NBA players in the Olympics; and in the 1992 Games in Barcelona, Spain, the likes of Magic Johnson and Larry Bird could be on the U.S. team.

College

Most colleges have basketball teams for men and women. They play about thirty games a season. Large crowds turn out, and many games are televised. The best college players are "drafted" by the pros, and many go on to successful careers in the NBA.

The leading college organization is the National College Athletic Association (NCAA). The goal of major teams is to qualify for the NCAA championship tournament at the end of the season. There are sixty-four teams that make it. This gets reduced to the "Sweet Sixteen" and then to "The Final Four."

National Basketball Association (NBA)

The NBA has 27 teams divided into four divisions: Central, Atlantic, Pacific, and Midwest. The Central and Atlantic make up the Eastern Conference, while the Pacific and Midwest are in the Western Conference. They play 82 regular-season games. Then, play-offs are held to see which two teams play for the NBA championship.

NBA teams have only twelve players on their rosters. This makes the NBA a very exclusive club with a total of only about 350 players. The average salary is over a half-million dollars a year. Top players earn well over $1 million a year.

Basketball Stars

Following are some of the game's greatest players, past and present:

Stars of the Past

George Mikan: Center for the Minneapolis Lakers who dominated the game from 1947 through 1954.

Bob Cousy: Smooth-playing Boston Celtics guard in the 1950s. He could make fancy passes look easy.

Oscar Robertson: "The Big O," he was a top scorer and playmaker for the Cincinnati Royals in the 1960s.

Jerry West: Top scorer and playmaker who starred for the Los Angeles Lakers in the 1960s.

Bill Russell: Top Boston Celtics center in the 1950s and 1960s who was known for his rebounding and defense.

Wilt Chamberlain: The greatest scorer ever, "Wilt the Stilt" averaged 30 points per game during his fourteen-year NBA career. In 1962, he set a record when he scored 100 points in a single game.

Elgin Baylor: Los Angeles Lakers forward who

49

was a top scorer in the 1960s. Agile player who used acrobatic moves under the basket.

Julius Irving: A fast and powerful forward in the 1970s and 1980s, Dr. J starred in both the ABA and NBA for the N. Y. Nets (now the New Jersey Nets). He seemed to have wings whenever he leaped to the hoop.

Kareem Abdul-Jabbar: Durable center for the Milwaukee Bucks and Los Angeles Lakers during the 1970s and 1980s who is the NBA's all-time scoring leader with 37,639 points.

Stars of the Present

Charles Barkley, Philadelphia 76ers: Muscular power forward with the stamina to play hard at the end of a game.

Larry Bird, Boston Celtics: A forward known for his all-around play and court savvy. A great shooter and passer. He can do it all on the court.

Earvin "Magic" Johnson, Los Angeles Lakers: Outstanding playmaker who has led L.A. to several NBA titles. At 6'9", he's taller than most guards but very quick and smooth.

Michael Jordan, Chicago Bulls: An unstoppable scorer who has become the game's most exciting and talked-about player.

Akeem "The Dream" Olajuwon, Houston Rockets: Top center who is one of the NBA's best rebounders. He is a native of Nigeria, in Africa.

Isiah Thomas, Detroit Pistons: Graceful guard whose playmaking led his team to the 1989 and 1990 NBA championship.

Chapter 8
Training Rules

Have you heard all the news about how kids today are out of shape? It's true. Doctors and researchers who study fitness have been testing young people to see what kind of shape they're in. If you're in good shape, you're probably in good health.

Unfortunately most of the news has been bad. Like most adults, kids don't seem to get enough exercise. Even kids involved in sports can barely run around the block without getting out of breath.

Young athletes cannot always depend on their sports play to keep them in tip-top condition. One reason is that most sports are not played year-round. For example, the basketball season runs only a few months. It's best to stay active twelve months a year.

The pros understand this. They know that the first rule of sports is: Use it or lose it. Any part of your body that you do not use regularly becomes weak. If you do no physical activity for a couple of weeks, you'll discover this.

Getting into shape requires time, effort, and patience. There are many guidelines for building your body for sports, staying in shape, and preventing injury. Being aware of them will help you in basketball and other sports as well. And you'll improve your health, too.

1. Shape up: You probably don't need to do much extra exercise during the basketball season. Practices and games should keep you active. At other times, try to ride a bicycle or swim or play volleyball a couple of times a week. Also, do some stretching exercises to stay loose.

2. Enjoy sports: Don't feel you have to win all the time. If you're relaxed about sports, you'll have more fun.

3. Variety is best: Even if you love basketball, try other sports, too, so you won't get bored. Many people who exercise now vary their activities. You may have friends or neighbors who run one day and ride a bike the next. This is known as "cross-training."

4. Eat properly: Your eating habits can affect how you feel during games and practices. For more on good nutrition for sports, see chapter 9.

5. Get enough rest: Young athletes should take a break from hard exercise. It's not healthy to play all-out day after day. Even the pros have days off. You also need plenty of sleep at night. If you have any difficulty sleeping, make sure you tell your parents.

6. Be patient: Getting in shape is a form of learning for your body. Just as you can't learn everything about math overnight, you can't develop your body overnight, either. There are no shortcuts.

As you get in shape, you could hit a plateau. For a while, it may seem like you're not making any progress. Then, suddenly, you'll find yourself improving. This is the body's way of getting used to physical activity.

7. Be specific: Your body gets fit in exact ways. For example, your shoulders are strengthened by swimming, and your legs are strengthened by running. Not all running is the same, either. For basketball, fast running works better than slow running because on the court you move in short, quick bursts.

8. Warm up: Always warm up before playing by stretching, dribbling, shooting, and passing the ball around.

9. Cool down: After a game, stretch a little more to "cool down." Your muscles will appreciate this the next day.

10. Don't skimp on drinks: Always take a water bottle to practices and games. Drink whenever you feel you need to, especially if it's warm. You sweat and get tired in the cold as well as the heat, so you must drink even when it's cold out.

Coaches usually allow you to drink as much as you want. There may be some coaches who punish players by not allowing them to drink. This is wrong. If it happens to you, tell your parents. They may have to discuss this with the coach or alert other basketball officials.

11. Getting strong: As you get in shape, you build strong muscles. In most sports, including basketball, quickness and the intelligent use of your body are more important than power. If you'd like to develop extra strength, do exercises like push-ups, sit-ups, and pull-ups. At your age, weight training is not necessary.

Chapter 9
Good Food

You've probably noticed that professional basketball players are not only strong, quick, and coordi-
nated, but they are also trim. They don't carry any
extra body fat around the court.

Being trim helps players move quickly. It also
enables them to last an entire game without becoming
exhausted. As experienced athletes, they've learned
that in addition to natural ability, there are two main
reasons for success in sports: practice and diet.

If you work hard at basketball, you'll improve
your skills. But if you don't eat properly, you won't be
able to use those skills to their utmost. You'll be slow
on the court. You'll be huffing and puffing after a fast
break.

Good food gives you energy and builds you up.
Food that is not very good for you clogs your system,
making you feel tired. It does not help you maintain
proper weight, either.

Many foods that are good for young athletes like
yourself also taste good. You probably eat some of
them already: spaghetti, pizza, turkey, apples,
oranges, bananas, baked potatoes, bagels, fruit juice.
Sounds pretty tasty, right?

Many people assume that foods like pizza are not
good for you. That is because they put toppings like

54

sausage and pepperoni on their pizza. Plain pizza usually is made of cheese, tomato sauce, and dough.
There's nothing unhealthy about that. If you smother
your pizza with vegetables such as pepper or mush-
rooms, that's okay, too.

However, sausage and pepperoni are high in fat.
There is also a lot of fat in "fast foods." Fat is the
wrong kind of fuel for your body. As an athlete, you
have to zip around like a sports car. Your body is like
an engine: It needs fuel.

People seem to be so busy nowadays they don't
have time to "eat to win." They gulp down burgers,
fries, and milk shakes. What you eat, and when you
eat it, should become a part of your overall sports
training. This is known as sports nutrition.

So far, you've seen these rules on eating for athletic activity:

(1) Pay attention to sports nutrition.

(2) Good foods build you up instead of slowing
you down.

(3) Good foods are tasty, too.

(4) Avoid foods that have a lot of fat.

There are other rules you should know about.

Have you heard the phrase "balanced diet"? Milk,
bread, meat, fish, fruits, and vegetables are some
foods that go into a balanced diet. You'd feel miser-
able if you ate only one kind of food all the time.

The fifth rule is: (5) Don't eat that much meat. Most
meat is high in fat. If you have meat every day, your
stomach may feel unsettled.

A type of meat that is less fatty is chicken or

turkey—as long as you don't smother it with a fatty gravy. You can't go wrong with a fresh turkey sandwich.

Just make sure you don't eat that sandwich right before playing basketball. This brings up the sixth rule: (6) Plan ahead.

If you don't plan your eating ahead of time, you could end up with a side pain during a basketball game. You've probably felt this type of pain during sports. It's known as a "stitch." Eating too close to a game can cause this to happen to you. So can eating fatty foods that are not easily digested.

Make sure you know when practices and games are scheduled. It's a good idea to eat at least two hours before exercise, even if you are having something light.

School lunches, which may fall close to sports play, must be handled with care. Have some fruit or a sandwich. It's better to feel a little hungry than stuffed before playing ball.

On weekends, if you play ball in the morning, your dinner the night before and breakfast that day—if you have one—become very important.

Should you eat the morning of a game? It depends. If you like to have breakfast, you'll have to get up extra early. Have something that goes down easy and gives energy. Some examples: a nutritional cereal with skim milk and sliced banana or other fruit, muffins, or yogurt. Make sure you drink, too—water, juice, or milk. Skip the doughnuts.

For sports, just about the best food you can eat is

a popular meal, and one already mentioned: spaghetti. Spaghetti, lasagna, ziti, and other noodle
dishes are all types of pasta. Pasta contains almost no
fat but plenty of carbohydrates. Your muscles love carbohydrates. They devour them for energy. Some people may think spaghetti is a fattening food. It is only
if you drown it with fatty sauces. Tomato sauce is best.
And don't load up on meatballs and sausage.

As you can guess, the seventh rule of eating for
sports is: (7) When in doubt, rely on pasta.

You've seen that many different types of foods are
good for you, and good-tasting, too. This leads to the
eighth and final rule: (8) Eat a variety of foods. No food
is totally "bad" for you as long as you don't make a
habit of it. Even Big Macs and Whoppers are okay
once in a while. Just make sure you don't eat one
before a big game.

Chapter 10
Setting Goals

How would you like to be able to steal the ball on defense, then race downcourt dribbling alternately with both hands, go up for a layup with defenders all over you, and make the basket?

Wouldn't that be a terrific accomplishment? Perhaps you've imagined yourself making a play like that some day. Top players can do it, and so can you.

Thinking about having the skills to make that kind of play is a type of goal. Most athletes have goals. Some goals may concern an upcoming game. Other goals may cover the entire season.

Oftentimes, one big goal can be broken up into smaller ones. Trying to achieve the small goals first will lead to the larger one.

Consider all that is involved in the steal-and-score play mentioned. It takes defense, dribbling, moving quickly with the ball, shooting, and being able to concentrate with other players around you.

If perfecting this play was your goal, you would plan to work on each of those skills separately. For example, it takes a lot of practice to be able to control the ball while dribbling on the run. You can't bounce the ball too high, or let it come too close to your body. You can't run too fast, or you'll run away from the ball. Your timing must be just right.

Once you can do that, you can advance to switching hands with the ball. That will enable you to maneuver around a defender who charges after you. Then, of course, you still have to make the basket.

Sound impossible? If you keep your goals high, you could do better than you might expect. That's what happened to high-scoring Felice Mann, a 5'9" guard at Burgard High in Buffalo, New York. In one 1990 game, Burgard was 22 points behind Traditional High with four minutes left to play.

It looked as if the game was over, but Mann would not give up. She began to bury shots from all over the court. She hit six 3-pointers. Burgard won in overtime. And Mann ended up with 73 points, a state record.

Why You Need Goals

You probably have goals all the time without realizing it. When you study for a test or do chores around the house, you certainly have goals in mind.

Goals keep you organized and focused on one thing at a time. They help you know your strengths and weaknesses.

If you're a skilled ball handler but have trouble rebounding, you'll need to concentrate on your efforts under the boards. Perhaps you're not getting into proper position, or you're jumping too soon. Better rebounding, then, should be a key goal for you.

Determining Your Goals

You'll be successful in basketball if you keep your

59

goals realistic. If you're assigned to guard a very good player, don't think, "He (or she) won't score any points off me." Tell yourself this, instead: "I'm going to play tight defense, follow the coach's instructions, and make my opponent work hard on every play."

Achieving Your Goals

In the pros, success does not come from physical ability alone. All players study the game in basketball "classes." They review films of previous games, jotting down notes, and learn plays that coaches teach.

Young players don't get a chance to look at game films. But you do learn plays and new skills all the time. You might learn something by watching a game on TV.

Collect what you learn about the sport and write it down in a basketball diary. Take an ordinary notebook, and set it up like a calendar. Each page could be a different day on which you play. Write down the details of practices and games so you'll be able to keep track of your progress and goals. You can even make note of your favorite pro players and how they're doing, too.

Don't be bashful about asking others for help. Parents, teachers, coaches, teammates, and friends can be called on for advice and encouragement.

Be patient. Concentrate on your primary goals. And, most of all, have as much fun as you can playing the great game of basketball.

Glossary

Basketball Talk

You've learned a lot of new words, names, and phrases that are part of the language of basketball. Here's a summary of key terms, in alphabetical order. Try to know them all.

assist: when a player passes to another player who then sinks a basket

backcourt: when the offense has the ball in the first half of the court, before the mid-court line

bank shot: a shot that hits the backboard before going into the basket

baseline: the out-of-bounds line underneath the basket

boxing out: using your body to keep an opponent behind you when positioning yourself for a rebound

center: tall player who takes position near the basket and is counted on for rebounds

defense: the team without the ball, trying to prevent the offensive team from scoring

double team: when two defensive players guard one offensive player

dribble: bouncing the ball to keep control of it before passing or shooting

dunk: making a basket by jumping high enough to put your hand over the rim with the ball

fast break: when the offensive team moves the ball quickly downcourt

field goal: a regular basket "from the floor" worth two or three points

Final Four: the NCAA Division I semifinal and final championship games for men and women

forward: player who is positioned mainly in the corners and is counted on for scoring and rebounding

foul shot: a free shot awarded when a team commits a foul, worth one point

free throw: another name for a foul shot

freeze: when a team does not shoot but keeps the ball by dribbling and passing for a long time

goaltending: when a defensive player blocks a shot that is close to the basket and looks like it will go in

guard: player who brings the ball upcourt, sets up plays, known as a playmaker

hang time: when a player can "hang" in midair while attempting a difficult shot

hook shot: extending your arm and shooting the ball over your head while looking at the basket

jump ball: play to start the game where the ball is thrown between two tall players who try to tap it to a teammate

jump shot: a shot made while jumping as opposed to standing still

layup: a shot made after dribbling up to the basket

National Basketball Association (NBA): the leading professional league in the U.S.

offense: the team that has the ball

outlet pass: the first pass thrown downcourt after a team gets possession of the ball

personal foul: a foul that gives the other team a free throw

physical fitness: doing exercise to get in shape

pivot: moving from side to side while keeping one foot still as a pivot

post: playing with your back to the basket to be in position to receive a pass

press: when the defense guards the offense closely, either from mid-court or when the ball is thrown into play

push shot: a shot taken while standing still, formerly called a set shot

rebound: getting possession of the ball after a missed shot

referee: official who enforces the rules during a game

screen: when an offensive player blocks a defender so that a teammate can get a better shot

set play: when the offense tries a specific play that was tried in practice

shot clock: the clock used to make sure a shot is taken within a specified period of time

technical foul: an extra free throw awarded when a player or coach shows poor sportsmanship

three-second rule: rule that prevents an offensive player from remaining in front of or very close to the basket for three or more seconds

throw-in: when the ball is thrown into play from the sidelines or behind the baseline

turnover: when the offense loses the ball because of a mistake or poor judgment

traveling: when a player with the ball takes an extra step while dribbling, also called walking

zone defense: instead of each player guarding another player (in one-to-one defense), the defense is assigned areas of the court

Appendix

NBA TEAM CHAMPIONS

1947: Philadelphia Warriors
1948: Baltimore Bullets
1949: Minneapolis Lakers
1950: Minneapolis Lakers
1951: Rochester Royals
1952: Minneapolis Lakers
1953: Minneapolis Lakers
1954: Minneapolis Lakers
1955: Syracuse Nationals
1956: Philadelphia Warriors
1957: Boston Celtics
1958: St. Louis Hawks
1959: Boston Celtics
1960: Boston Celtics
1961: Boston Celtics
1962: Boston Celtics
1963: Boston Celtics
1964: Boston Celtics
1965: Boston Celtics
1966: Boston Celtics
1967: Philadelphia 76ers
1968: Boston Celtics

1969: Boston Celtics
1970: New York Knicks
1971: Milwaukee Bucks
1972: Los Angeles Lakers
1973: New York Knicks
1974: Boston Celtics
1975: Golden State Warriors
1976: Boston Celtics
1977: Portland Trailblazers
1978: Washington Bullets
1979: Seattle Supersonics
1980: Los Angeles Lakers
1981: Boston Celtics
1982: Los Angeles Lakers
1983: Philadelphia 76ers
1984: Boston Celtics
1985: Los Angeles Lakers
1986: Boston Celtics
1987: Los Angeles Lakers
1988: Los Angeles Lakers
1989: Detroit Pistons
1990: Detroit Pistons

BASKETBALL ORGANIZATIONS

For further information, contact these groups:

Biddy Youth Basketball
4711 Bancroft Drive
New Orleans, LA 70122
(504) 288-5128

National Federation
of State High School
Athletic Associations
11724 Plaza Circle
P.O. Box 20626
Kansas City, MO 64195
(816) 464-5400

National Basketball
Association
645 Fifth Avenue
New York, NY 10022
(212) 826-7000

National Collegiate
Athletic Association
Nall Avenue at 63rd Street
P.O. Box 1906
Mission, KS 66201
(913) 384-3220

Further Reading

Basketball's Greatest Stars, by Al Hirshberg (Putnam's, 1963)

Basketball for Young Champions, by Robert J. Antonacci and Jene Barr (McGraw-Hill, 1979)

Better Basketball for Girls, by George Sullivan (Dodd, Mead, 1978)

How to Play Better Basketball, by C. Paul Jackson (Crowell, 1968)

The Game of Basketball, by Guernsey Van Riper, Jr. (Garrard, 1967)

The Story of Basketball, by Dave Anderson (Morrow, 1988)

About the Author

Marc Bloom writes on health, fitness, and sports for *The New York Times*, *Runner's World* magazine, *American Health*, and other publications. He lives in Marlboro, New Jersey, with his wife and two daughters, both of whom are active in sports.

Other Books by Marc Bloom
Cross-Country Running
The Marathon
Olympic Gold
The Runner's Bible